U.S. Fish & Wildlife Service

Sport Fish and Wildlife Restoration

Program Update February 2001

I0439685

The mission of the U.S. Fish & Wildlife Service is working with others to conserve, protect and enhance fish and wildlife and their habitats for the continuing benefit of the American people.

The overall mission of the Federal Aid Program is to:

"Strengthen the ability of State and Territorial fish and wildlife agencies to restore and manage fish and wildlife resources to meet effectively the consumptive and nonconsumptive needs of the public for fish and wildlife resources."

Message from the Assistant Director for Migratory Birds and State Programs

The past two years were tumultuous for the Federal Aid in Sport Fish and Wildlife Restoration Programs. After decades as the silent centerpiece of our nation's fish and game conservation efforts, the program came under an unprecedented level of scrutiny. I am speaking specifically about the results of 18 months of audits and evaluations. Recently, Congress passed the Wildlife and Sport Fish Restoration Programs Improvement Act of 2000 (Act), providing guidance on how the Service administers the Federal Aid Programs. This legislation establishes a basis on which we will build even greater success.

The Act specifies a dozen tasks considered necessary for the administration of the Federal Aid Programs. It sets expenditures for administration at $18 million for two years. Available funds decrease in subsequent years. We are realigning our activities and staffing to meet the direction and funding defined in the Act. The legislation establishes a new firearm and bowhunter education and safety program grant, and a Multi-State grant program to reach across State and Regional boundaries to address environmental needs. The Act also provides $900,000 to administer the various non-formula grant programs including the Clean Vessel Act, the Outreach and Communications Program operated by the Recreational Boating and Fishing Foundation, the Partnerships for Wildlife Program, and others. Finally, the Act funds the Marine State Fisheries Commissions and the Sport Fish and Boating Partnership Council to enhance aquatic conservation efforts and partnerships among industry, constituency groups, and government.

Prior to the Act, the Service and our partners created Federal Aid improvement teams to examine the administrative issues identified during previous evaluations. During the past year, these teams have analyzed our processes and our responsibilities. The upshot of these process improvement initiatives will be more consistent, more responsive, and more reliable Sport Fish and Wildlife Restoration Programs. I am proud to report that we have already implemented many recommendations. Ultimately, our goal is to continue the Federal Aid Program's legacy to viable resources and programs.

The following report describes the activities the Division of Federal Aid engaged in during fiscal year 2000. The information provided does not incorporate the impacts of the Act. The Division will produce another issue of the Program Updates during 2001 providing information on the effects of the Act.

The future holds a period of improvements and changes in the Division of Federal Aid. It has been a long, trying road for the Program and the staff but with renewed vigor we will see the Federal Aid in Sport Fish and Wildlife Restoration Programs rebound. I assure you that the Sport Fish and Wildlife Restoration Programs will remain reliable and valuable.

Table of Contents

Division of Federal Aid Washington Office Staff Directory

Division of Federal Aid
Washington Office
4401 N. Fairfax Drive
Suite 140
Arlington, VA 22203
Main: 703/358 2156
Fax: 703/358 1837

Internet Home Page:
http://fa.r9.fws.gov

*Kris E. LaMontagne, Chief

*Larry Bandolin, Deputy Chief

Vacant
Division Chief Secretary

*Gary Reintz, Branch Chief
Policy Development and Deployment

Jack Hicks, Policy Development
Specialist

Steve Farrell,
Small Grants Project Leader
National Outreach Coordinator

Tim Hess,
Policy Development Specialist

Michael Vanderford,
Policy Development Specialist

Vacant
Aquatic Resource Education
Hunter Education
Shooting Range Program

Steve Leggans,
Training Coordinator

*Tom Jeffrey, Branch Chief
Budget and Administration

Mary Jones,
Administration Officer

Pete Peterson,
Program Support Assistant

Michelle Morman,
Administrative Technician

Jimmye Kane,
Secretary

*Bill Conlin, Branch Chief
Information Resources & ADP
Management.

Jeffrey Graves,
Computer Specialist

David Washington,
Computer Specialist

Lanny Moore,
Audits & Cash Management

Bill Gruber,
Audit Program Specialist

*Sylvia Cabrera, Branch Chief
Hunting, Fishing and Wildlife-
Associated Recreation Survey

Richard Aiken,
Economist
Survey Specialist

Genevieve Pullis,
Economist
Survey Specialist

Blake Weirich,
Assistant Training Coordinator

Luther Zachary,
FAIMS Fish & Wildlife Biologist

Dale Beaumariage,
FAIMS Education Specialist

C. J. Huang,
FAIMS Database Administrator

Pete Hitchcock,
FAIMS Network Engineer

Denotes managers

The Federal Aid in Sport Fish Restoration Program

Background and History

The Federal Aid in Sport Fish Restoration (SFR) Program serves as a model user-pays, user-benefits program. As enacted into law in 1950, the SFR Act (also called the Dingell-Johnson Act for its congressional sponsors) applied a 10% manufacturer's excise tax on fishing rods, reels, creels, and artificial baits, lures, and flies. The U.S. Treasury collected the taxes, transferring the revenue to the Fish and Wildlife Service (prior to the creation of the Aquatic Resources Trust Fund in 1984) as a permanent, indefinite appropriation. The Service distributed SFR funds to the States and Insular Territories to fund projects enhancing sport fish restoration efforts.

The Service bases State's share of these two-year funds 60% on its number of licensed anglers and 40% on its land and water area. No State may receive more than 5% or less than 1% of each year's total apportionment. Puerto Rico receives 1%, and the Virgin Islands, Guam, American Samoa, Northern Mariana Islands, and the District of Columbia each receive one-third of 1%. Except in the Insular Territories, grantees may use Federal funds for up to 75% of the cost of SFR projects providing remaining funds from a State match.

Before apportioning SFR funds to the States, the Service deducts up to 6% to administer the program. The Service uses these funds to assure compliance with the SFR Act, provide technical assistance, and set performance standards. Up to $2.5 million of these funds are also available annually for outreach and communication projects as specified in the Transportation Equity Act for the 21st Century (TEA21). Each Sate independently selects, plans, and performs the necessary project work.

In 1984, then Representative John Breaux of Louisiana and Senator Malcolm Wallop of Wyoming lead Congress in extending the tax to include tackle boxes and other recreational fishing equipment. A 3% tax was applied to electric trolling motors and flasher-type sonar fish finders. The amendment also established import duties on fishing tackle and pleasure boats. The Wallop-Breaux Amendment also required States to use a minimum of 10% (now 15% due to TEA21) of SFR apportionments for motorboat access and up to 10% for aquatic education. The amendment required Coastal States to distribute "new monies" from the 1984 amendments equitably among fresh and saltwater projects. This wording was changed to include all appropriations going to coastal States in 1988. In addition, the amendment identified a portion of the existing Federal tax on motorboat fuels to be deposited in the newly created ARTF from which the Service funds the SFR Program and the Boating Safety Account. The Wallop-Breaux Amendment increased SFR funding from $38,085,995 in 1985 to $109,959,300 in1986. In many States, SFR funds represent more than half the entire State's fishery budget.

The passage of TEA21 reaffirmed Congressional support for this model user-pay, user-benefit program. TEA21 changes in this program include provision of $5 million to be available for a new Outreach and Communications Program to improve communications with anglers, boaters and the general public. Congress created the outreach and communications program to reduce barriers to participation, advance adoption of sound fishing and boating practices, promote conservation and the responsible use of the Nation's aquatic resources, and to further safety in fishing and boating. Funding for this program will increase by $1 million annually until 2003 when Program funding will increase to $10 million.

TEA21 earmarked the SFR account to provide additional funds for State boating safety programs ($64 million for FY 1999) and for a competitive grant program to construct pumpout facilities for disposal of human waste from recreational boats ($10 million for FY 1999 through 2003). The minimum percentage of State allocations for boating access and facilities projects was increased from 12.5 percent to 15 percent for each State. Also, the States are provided five years in which to obligate their boating access monies.

Starting in 2000 and continuing through 2003, $8 million will be available annually for qualified projects under the new Boating Infrastructure Grant Program. This program provides funds to States for the development and maintenance of public facilities such as slips, mooring buoys, day docks and navigational aids for transient nontrailerable (over 26 feet in length) recreational vessels.

Motorboat fuels taxes transferred to the Aquatic Resources Trust Fund (ARTF) before October 1, 2005, will increase by a projected $151 million. Currently, the amount of Federal gasoline tax transferred to the ARTF, representing fuel used by boaters, is calculated using 11.5 cents per gallon of gas. On October 1, 2001, this figure will increase to 13 cents per gallon of gas, and on October 1, 2003 through October 1, 2005, the figure will be 13.5 cents. Consequently, States will receive an additional $151 million before October 1, 2005, increasing the total motorboat fuel taxes transferred to the ARTF for the seven-year period to $1.2 billion.

In 1990, Congress passed the Coastal Wetlands Planning, Protection, and Restoration Act to acquire, restore, and enhance coastal wetlands (only coastal States and Insular Territories are eligible). This Act transfers a percentage of the Federal gasoline tax based on use of gasoline by "small engines" through the ARTF to the

SFR Account. The Service distributes an amount equal to these funds or 18% of SFR receipts for a given year (whichever is greater) annually as follows: 1) 70% to the Louisiana Coastal Wetlands Restoration Program; 2) 15% to support the North American Wetlands Conservation Act; and 3) 15% to the National Coastal Wetlands Conservation Grants Program. TEA21 extended this program through 2005.

The impact the SFR Program has had on sport fishing nationwide is huge. Over the past 50 years, total State apportionments under the SFR Program have been more than $3.3 billion. These funds have helped to build or reclaim more than 4,082 boating access sites; to purchase or improve over 593,000 acres for boating and fishing; and to fund research and inventory projects resulting in better ways to manage fish populations.

Aquatic Resource Education

Aquatic education programs help people understand, enjoy and conserve natural resources. With the passage of TEA21 (Transportation Equity Act for the 21st Century) Congress raised the 10 percent cap on a State's use of Sport Fish Restoration dollars for aquatic education to 15 percent and applied the cap to outreach and communications projects. Although funding for aquatic education is optional, some 43 States, the District of Columbia and all the Insular Territories choose to spend some of their dollars on education. In 1998, they spent more than $11 million of Sport Fish Restoration funds on these programs.

Aquatic education programs are diverse and States tailor programs to their specific aquatic resource and citizen needs. The programs provide a hands-on, field-oriented approach to education and strive to offer educational opportunities to audiences across the State. Using such methods as workshops, curriculum support, volunteer-led clinics, and summer programs, States reach teachers, school students (K-12 and college), youth groups enrolled in recreation programs, urban youth and families, landowners, and visitors to State hatcheries, aquariums and education centers. Program topics vary but may cover freshwater, marine and estuarine ecology, watersheds, functions and values of wetlands, fisheries biology and management, and fishing skills, safety and ethics. Aquatic education programs give non-anglers, especially youth, the skills and opportunities to make fishing a lifetime pursuit. Some programs include issue investigation and critical thinking skills training and incorporate action projects contributing to the development of stewardship behavior.

To stretch dollars and expertise, States use partnerships, including colleges and universities, other state resource and education agencies, local recreation departments, tackle manufacturers and retailers, community groups, city youth organizations, summer camps, and local and national conservation organizations. In recent years, many States have tied their programs to new state education and student performance standards, increasing their use in schools. States also use evaluation research to strengthen all aspects of their aquatic education programs.

Boating Infrastructure Grant Program

The Sportfishing and Boat Safety Act of 1998 authorized 1) a competitive grant program for States to develop and maintain facilities for transient nontrailerable (over 26 feet in length) recreational boats; and 2) a national framework for a public boat access needs assessment that States may use to conduct surveys to determine the adequacy of facilities providing access for all recreational boats. The Act authorizes a competitive grant program to States for the cost of constructing, renovating and maintaining facilities for transient nontrailerable recreational boats. The $32 million grant program ($8 million per year) began in the year 2000 and will end in 2003. The Federal government will pay up to 75 percent of the cost with States or other partners matching the remaining 25 percent. Proposals submitted in accordance with a State plan, providing for public/private partnership efforts, and providing for innovative ways to increase the availability of facilities receive priority consideration.

The Service will complete development of the national framework by the spring of 2001. States may use the framework to survey facilities providing access for all recreational boats, and to determine the future needs. States may fund surveys from allocations for motorboat access. States do not have to complete a survey to earn preference if the Secretary of the Interior certifies that they are carrying out a plan ensuring adequate public boating access.

Clean Vessel Act Pumpout Grant Program

Congress passed the Clean Vessel Act (CVA) in 1992 to help reduce pollution from recreational vessel sewage discharges. The Act established a five-year grant program authorizing $40 million from the Sport Fish Restoration Account for use by the States. Federal funds make up 75% of all approved projects. The TEA21 reauthorized the CVA in 1998, providing $50 million over five years ending in fiscal year 2003. Since 1992, the CVA has funded the installation of over 3,500 pumpout stations and more than 2,000 dump stations. During fiscal year 2000, the Service issued $10.6 million in CVA grants to 33 States and two Territories.

Grants are available on a competitive basis for the construction, operation, and maintenance of pumpout and portable toilet dump stations. Priorities for awarding grants are given to proposals from coastal States with an approved pumpout plan, providing public/private partnerships, using innovative techniques to increase availability and use of pumpout stations, incorporating an education component, benefitting waters affected by sewage discharge, and occurring in areas with low vessel/pumpout station ratios.

States submit grant proposals each year to Regional Offices for review and submission to the Washington Office. The Service convenes a panel of Federal employees including representatives from the Service's Washington Office, the National Oceanic and Atmospheric Administration, the Environmental Protection Agency, and the U.S. Coast Guard. The panel reviews the proposals, making funding recommendations to the Director of the Service.

Program guidance can be found in the Code of Federal Regulations (50 CFR 85). The Service published technical guidelines (information on appropriate types of facilities, surveys, plans, and education), and grant guidelines (information on how to apply for grants) in the Federal Register on March 10, 1994. Guidelines on requirements for a uniform pumpout symbol, slogan and program crediting were published in the Federal Register on August 27, 1997.

Coastal Wetlands Planning, Protection, and Restoration Program

The Coastal Wetlands Planning, Protection and Restoration Act made funds available by allocating 18 percent of the Sport Fish Restoration Account or 100 percent of the excise tax on small engine fuels (whichever is greater) for the protection of these fragile areas. Of the 18 percent allocated, the program provides 15 percent (not to exceed $15 million) for the National Coastal Wetlands Conservation Grant Program.

The Director of the Fish & Wildlife Service administers the Coastal Wetlands Conservation Grant Program. The Division of Federal Aid and the Division of Fish and Wildlife Management Assistance and Habitat Restoration conduct a cross-program review of project proposals. All Coastal States (except Louisiana) and the Trust Territories are eligible to submit project proposals to the appropriate Service Regional Office annually.

Through the Coastal Wetlands Conservation Grant Program, the Fish and Wildlife Service makes $10 to $15 million available annually. Results of the last four years are shown here:

FY	# of proposals	Cost	Acres
1998	20	$9.8M	12,680
1999	18	$9.8M	24,900
2000	25	$11.8M	5,500
2001	22	$15M	11,350

A total of 25 different coastal States and one Territory received funding under this program between 1992 and 2001, for a total of 181 projects. Project participants in this program are generally State and Territorial agencies but have included State, county and municipal governments and non-government partners as well. For the $90 million granted, approximately 105,000 acres have or will be protected and/or restored.

Congress reauthorized The Coastal Wetlands Planning, Protection and Restoration Act in November, 2000 through fiscal year 2009.

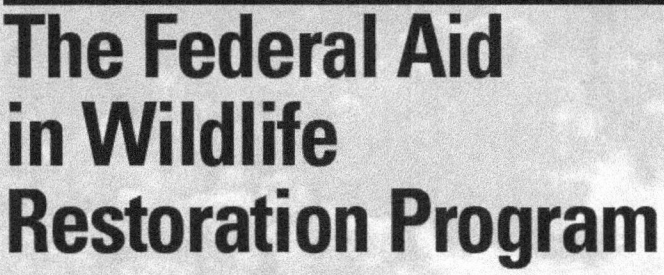

The Federal Aid in Wildlife Restoration Program

Background and History

The Federal Aid in Wildlife Restoration Program began functioning July 1, 1938, following passage of the Federal Aid in Wildlife Restoration Act by Congress. The U.S. Fish and Wildlife Service administers this Act (also known as the Pittman-Robertson Act after its sponsors).

Funds are derived from a Federal excise tax on the manufacture of arms and ammunition, including handguns, and on archery equipment. These taxes are collected from the manufacturers by the Department of Treasury and allocated to the Fish and Wildlife Service. Based on a formula set forth in the Act, the Service apportions these funds to the 50 States, the Commonwealth of Puerto Rico, Guam, American Samoa, the Northern Mariana Islands, and the Virgin Islands. This formula provides for the apportionment, based on one-half of the ratio which the area of each State bears to the total area of all the States, and one-half on the ratio which the number of paid hunting license holders of each State bears to the total number of paid license holders of all the States.

In the early 1970's, Congress expanded the Act's revenue base to include handguns and archery equipment. Congress also authorized States to spend up to one-half of those apportioned funds on hunter education and shooting ranges. Congress has based the apportionment of these new revenues only on the population of each State.

Responsibility for selection, planning, and execution of wildlife restoration projects rests with the States, through their designated wildlife management agency. The Federal government may reimburse states for up to 75 percent of the total costs of approved projects. Financial aid under this Act is not available to private clubs, local or county governments, or individuals, except from State agencies for such projects as they approve.

The designated State agencies submit project proposals to the Regional Directors of the FWS for approval. Projects may include acquisition of areas of land or water for feeding, resting, or as breeding places for wildlife; rehabilitation or improvement, by construction or otherwise, of land or water areas for the benefit of wildlife, such as wildlife management areas, public hunting areas and sportsmen's facilities; regular maintenance of completed projects; management of wildlife resources (exclusive of law enforcement or public relations activities); research into the problems of wildlife management; hunter safety courses and construction of target ranges; and coordination of projects necessary to the efficient administration affecting wildlife resources.

Hunter Education— Shooting Range Program

An amendment to the Federal Aid in Wildlife Restoration Act on October 23, 1970 included provision for hunter training programs and the development, operation and maintenance of public shooting ranges. Funding for hunter education and shooting ranges is derived from one-half of the 11 percent excise tax on archery equipment and the 10 percent excise tax on handguns, pistols and revolvers. States use the other one-half of the tax money for wildlife restoration purposes.

The Service distributes this money based on population of a State compared to other States with a maximum apportionment of 3 percent and a minimum of 1 percent. Guam, Northern Mariana Islands, American Samoa and the Virgin Islands each receive one-sixth of 1 percent of the total hunter education funds.

State hunter education programs include the development and implementation of a programmed course of instruction leading toward the achievement of a State's hunter education goals and objectives. States design the course to train students to be safe and responsible hunters, and help State agencies in accomplishing their mission and goals.

The Service may approve advanced hunter education training if it offers hunters an opportunity to enhance their knowledge of safe and legal hunting practices. The primary objective of all advanced courses will address specific individual State hunter education needs. For example, the State may want to provide special training for elk hunters to decrease populations of elk in certain areas.

The backbone of the hunter education program is the cadre of more than 45,000 volunteer instructors. Volunteers contribute approximately $30 million worth of services annually.

States are encouraged to develop or enter third-party agreements to gain a suitable number of safe shooting and archery facilities. To provide this hands-on experience, the States may lease or rent archery and shooting range facilities or services from local clubs.

In fiscal year 2000, the Fish and Wildlife Service apportioned $29,201,362 to States and Territories (except Puerto Rico) for use in hunter education activities.

Partnerships for Wildlife Program

Three fourths of all American children and adults participate in wildlife-related recreational activities other than hunting, fishing and trapping. More than 80 percent of vertebrate fish and wildlife species in North America are not harvested for human use. Representatives of these same species continue to be added to the list of endangered and threatened species at an alarming rate.

Recognizing that many States could no longer afford to conserve the entire array diverse fish and wildlife species, Congress passed the Partnerships for Wildlife Act (P.L. 102-587, Title VII) which President Bush signed into law on November 4, 1992. On October 30, 1998, Congress reauthorized the Act through 2003..

The purpose of the Partnerships for Wildlife Act is to establish partnerships between the Service, State fish and wildlife agencies, and private organizations and individuals to preserve and manage all nongame fish and wildlife species. The Act authorizes grants to States (only eligible grant recipients) to benefit a broad array of nongame fish and wildlife species and to provide nonconsumptive fish and wildlife recreation opportunities. Funding is normally provided by contributions of 1/3 Federal, 1/3 State, and 1/3 private party.

Game species, endangered or threatened species, and marine mammals do not qualify for funding.

The FY 2000 Service budget made available $764,200 from appropriated Federal funds to be matched by equal amounts from State and private parties for 33 Partnerships for Wildlife grants.

A panel consisting of State, National Fish and Wildlife Foundation, and Service representatives will review projects received in FY 2001 and recommend those for funding to the Director by March of 2001.

Partnerships for Wildlife Projects Funded for Fiscal Year 2000

State	Title	Federal Share	Running Total
AZ	Conservation and management zones: Developing an alternative approach to conservation and management of native ranid frogs	$32,000	$32,000
CA	Demographic characteristics of Burrowing Owl populations	$20,000	$52,000
ME	Assessment of habitat and population status of the black tern in Maine	$22,768	$74,768
WI	Development of guidelines to prevent excessive mortality to bats using the largest known bat hibernaculum in the midwest—Neda Mine State Natural Area, WI	$5,000	$79,768
WI	Using field studies and GIS applications to model common loon resource selection and to identify factors limiting productivity on the breeding grounds in Wisconsin	$12,600	$92,368
WA	Reintroduce endangered Western Pond Turtles to new sites in the Columbia River Gorge and Puget Sound	$15,000	$107,368
FL	Volunteer program for management of conservation lands on Florida's Lake Wales Ridge	$50,000	$157,368
WI	Prairie insect distribution, status, and response to management	$90,000	$247,368
MO	Cooperative bird conservation area management	$30,000	$277,368
GA	Survey for Swallow-tailed Kite nests in the South Atlantic coastal plain of Georgia	$1,500	$278,868
OR	Restoration of grassland habitat on private and public lands Willamette Valley Province, Oregon	$20,000	$298,868
NJ	Identification, delineation, and faunal surveys of vernal pools in NJ	$44,000	$342,868
OR	Implementation of wildlife habitat conservation program in the Willamette Valley Province, Oregon	$21,000	$363,868
AZ	Arizona Desert Tortoise research and management	$43,000	$406,868
WI	Integrating livestock production and conservation: Use of cattle in the restoration of Oak Savannas	$31,383	$438,251
CA	Estimating breeding population size and developing long-term monitoring techniques for Zantus Murrelets	$12,000	$450,251
HI	Kaena Point Seabird Habitat Restoration Project	$50,000	$500,251

continued

Partnerships for Wildlife Projects Funded for Fiscal Year 2000 (continued)

State	Title	Federal Share	Running Total
GA	Friends of feathered flyers: Partners in flight bird activity boxes	$1,500	$501,751
WA	Living with Washington's Wildlife: A Four Part Approach	$5,000	$506,751
NJ	Full implementation of NJ Herp Atlas Project	$33,400	$540,151
WA	Effects of controlled timber harvest on the ecology of Western Grey Squirrels	$20,000	$560,151
WI	Grassland bird nesting success in lowland and upland pastures	$15,000	$575,151
WI	Establish prairie nursery beds for Hogback Prairie State Natural Area	$2,000	$577,151
MO	Cooperative bird survey	$20,000	$597,151
NY	Amphibian and reptile Atlas of NY state	$26,000	$623,151
IL	Metapopulation dynamics of Yellow-headed Blackbirds in Illinois	$6,752	$629,903
WI	Prairie, savanna and oak woodland restoration on Mississippi River Bluff State natural areas	$20,000	$649,903
WI	Landscape scale management of grassland bird populations in WI	$30,000	$679,903
WI	Factors influencing avian nesting success in Pine Barrens Savanna	$14,800	$694,703
NE	Publication of *The Mussels of Nebraska*	$21,959	$716,662
WI	Landscape management for prairie chickens in WI	$25,000	$741,662
NY	NY state breeding bird atlas 2000: *Block Busting*	$6,000	$747,662
KY	Neotropical migrant songbird monitoring, research, and management project in Kentucky, with emphasis on cooperative initiatives in the interior low plateau and Northern Cumberland plateau physiographic provinces.	$73,000	$820,662[1]

[1] *Carryover funds from FY 1999 identified after the selection of FY 2000 grants were made available for eligible projects.*

Activities Funded
With Federal Aid
Administrative Dollars

The National Survey of Fishing, Hunting, and Wildlife-Associated Recreation

2001 FHWAR SURVEY

April 2001, the Bureau of Census will begin data collection for the 2001 National Survey of Fishing, Hunting, and Wildlife-Associated Recreation. It will be the 10th FHWAR Survey sponsored by the U.S. Fish and Wildlife Service since 1955. The Service conducts it about every five years at the request of the State fish and wildlife agencies. The survey has become one of the Nation's most important sources of information on wildlife-related recreation participation and expenditures.

In March 1999, the FHWAR survey grants-in-aid subcommittee of the International Association of Fish and Wildlife Agencies recommended that the Service conduct the survey in 2001. The subcommittee recommended conducting a survey comparable to the 1991 & 1996 surveys to maintain trend information; increasing the sample sizes to recapture some State-level data lost when we reduced samples; and that the Bureau of Census conducts the Survey. The recommended funding level was $12.5 million. Due to funding constraints, the Service has budgeted only $10.2 million for the 2001 Survey. Although this means that the Service cannot increase sample sizes, the survey estimates will be comparable to the 1996 survey.

In June 1999, the Service signed an agreement with Census to conduct the 2001 survey. Census' 1,000 interviewers will collect the information through computer-assisted interviews. Interviewers will conduct the survey primarily by telephone. Interviewers will conduct in-person interviews when necessary. About 80,000 households will be contacted to identify samples of sportsmen (anglers and hunters) and wildlife watchers (wildlife feeders, observers, and photographers). Interviewers will ask these individuals about their activities and expenditures in 2001 in three different detailed interview waves.

The Service staff met with State technical committee members and non-governmental organizations to determine survey content. The Service also obtained input from Federal agencies, researchers, and other major survey users. On September 18, 2000, the Office of Management and Budget approved the Service's request to conduct the 2001 Survey.

Future important milestones include the following:

■ April-June 2001, Census will conduct screening interviews and the first Detailed Interview Wave.

■ September–October 2001, Census will conduct the second Detailed Interview Wave.

■ January–March 2002, Census will conduct the third Detailed Interview Wave. Data collection for the 2001 survey will be completed in mid-March.

■ July 2002, we will begin publishing preliminary estimates on participation and expenditures for fishing, hunting, and wildlife-associated recreation.

■ November 2002 the Service will publish the final National Report, and December 2002 we will begin to publish the State reports.

Survey products will include two preliminary reports, a final National and 50 State reports, technical reports, a CD-ROM, and a quick facts brochure. Reports will be accessible on the internet.

1996 FHWAR SURVEY

Information on the 1996 FHWAR Survey reports is available on the Service's home page at the following address: Http://fa.r9.fws.gov/surveys/surveys.html

Management Assistance Team

The Service established the Management Assistance Team to assist natural resource professionals in meeting a wide range of management challenges. In 1999, the MAT completed a formal rechartering effort led by a cross-section of MAT stakeholders. The group provided a set of recommendations focused on the function, clientele, and funding to the Director of the Service. Following review of the recommendations, the Service moved MAT to the National Conservation Training Center (NCTC) in Sherperdstown, WV. The Nation's premier site for fish and wildlife conservation education, NCTC shares a common goal with MAT to use new skills, share perspectives, and break down barriers to solve natural resource issues.

During fiscal year 2000, MAT continued to serve the State natural resource professionals to meet a variety of management challenges. MAT provided leadership development workshops to the Nevada and Utah Divisions of Wildlife helping both advance improved personnel initiatives. As a service to all of the State agencies, MAT completed work with the International Association of Fish and Wildlife Agencies and NCTC by producing a national diversity broadcast (Diversity: Key to the Future) featuring General Colin Powell. This was the first satellite down-link broadcast to all State fish and wildlife agencies. Continuing efforts to advance improved management, MAT helped the Pennsylvania Game Commission with agency-wide evaluation efforts and consulted with Puerto Rico on comprehensive management. Finally, MAT developed and conducted a strategic marketing workshop for the Alabama Department of Conservation and Natural Resources.

Fish and Wildlife Reference Service

The number of documents indexed during the 2000 Fiscal Year increased from 1,306 to 1,565 for the main bibliographic database and decreased from 788 to 479 documents for the Survey/Inventory database. Indexers, Geoffrey Yeadon and Jason Fish, continue processing proceedings of the Southeastern Association of Fish and Wildlife Agencies, finishing volumes from 1991 back to 1987. In addition, they indexed the last 300 reports from the series, Special Scientific Reports - Fisheries.

The total number of Cooperator pages photocopied was approximately 17,400 pages, less than the 1999 Fiscal Year. This decrease in the FWRS workload is reflected by the 3.5% fewer pages photocopied in FY 2000 than in FY 1999, and 5.9% fewer Cooperator orders processed. Thus, there may be a leveling of the trend of fewer orders received at the Reference Service. December was the busiest month of the 2000 Fiscal Year with FWRS clerical staff processing almost 1100 document orders. The orders required more than 81,000 pages of photocopies and 663 pages of microfiche while mailing out 2758 documents.

As of this report date, the FWRS databases contain 31,206 records in the Main Bibliographic database, 7734 records in the Survey/Inventory database, 322 records in the Boating Access database, 118 records in the Northeast Region's Black Bass database, 100 records in the Clean Vessel Act database, and 202 records in the new Habitat Conservation Plan database. In addition, our book database now stands at 434 titles of books stored at the FWRS facility.

FWRS published four newsletters in FY 2000. The number of copies printed and mailed, and the mailing dates and dates of first orders received are presented in Table 1. Mailing dates approximate those of FY 1999, except the Fall and Summer Newsletters, NL's 122 and 123 respectively, were mailed about one week later than the Fall and Summer Newsletters in FY 1999, and we mailed the Winter NL 123 earlier.

FWRS Newsletters sent and printed during Fiscal Year 2000

Newsletter Number	122	123	124	125
Cooperators	6929	7008	7130	7173
Clients	3144	3226	3353	3381
Canadian	327	333	334	327
Other Foreign	109	117	122	115
Total # Sent	10,509	10,684	10,939	10,996
Total # Printed	11,000	11,100	11,500	11,000
NL Mail Date	11/24/99	02/10/00	05/22/00	08/16/00

FWRS technical staff attended seven professional meetings during fiscal year 2000 (Table 2). We paid exhibitor fees for all meetings except the Natural Resources Information Council and the Association for Conservation Information conferences, which were small technical meetings for information and education personnel and natural resource librarians.

The total number of literature searches conducted continues to decline, down to 26 Cooperator searches from the 49 conducted in fiscal year 1999. We had predicted two years ago that the availability of all FWRS databases on our website would affect the numbers of searches run by the FWRS staff, and that continues to hold true in fiscal year 2000.

For the majority of Cooperator orders, document delivery turnaround times varied from 24 hours to a maximum of four days throughout the year 2000 fiscal year. Thus, the average turnaround times decreased some in fiscal year 2000.

Sport Fishing and Boating Partnership Council

The Sport Fishing and Boating Partnership Council (SFBPC) serves as a unique adviser to the Secretary of the Interior and the Director of the U.S. Fish and Wildlife Service. The Council, formed in January 1993, represents the interests of the public and private sectors of the sport fishing and boating communities. The Service has organized the Council to enhance partnerships among industry, constituency groups and government.

The Council is re-chartered every two years under the Federal Advisory Committee Act. Its membership of up to 18 people includes the Director of the Service and the president of the International Association of Fish and Wildlife Agencies, who both serve in ex officio capacities. Other Council members are directors from State agencies responsible for managing recreational fish and wildlife resources and individuals who represent the interests of saltwater and freshwater recreational fishing, recreational boating, the recreational fishing and boating industries, recreational fisheries resources conservation, aquatic resource outreach and education, and tourism.

In its most recent activities, the Council in September 2000 provided the U.S. Fish and Wildlife Service with "Saving a System in Peril," a report that outlines the Council's vision for strengthening the National Fish Hatchery System. A Council subcommittee consisting of 23 fisheries experts wrote the report. This unprecedented consensus within the fisheries community was reached after a year-long effort.

In addition, the SFBPC continues to monitor the progress in carrying out the "Strategic Plan for a National Outreach and Communications Program," designed by the Council to stimulate interest and participation in fishing, boating and aquatic resource stewardship. The nonprofit Recreational Boating and Fishing Foundation is implementing the plan, receiving $36 million over five years through the Sport Fish Restoration Program. The Council's continuing responsibilities with this project include reporting to the Secretary on stakeholders' responses to the plan's implementation.

More information about the SFBPC can be found on the Internet at http://www.sfbpc.fws.gov or by contacting Council Coordinator Laury Parramore at 703/358 2541 or e-mail laury_parramore@fws.gov.

Federal Aid Audit Program

The Federal Aid Audit Program has completed 31 audits, with an additional five audits completed in draft and 17 audits in progress. The status of audits is presented below with the anticipated completion dates for the audits in draft status. Additionally, a summary of trends and weaknesses noted in completed and ongoing audits follows.

Completed Audits	AK, AM SAM, AR, CA, CO, CT, FL, FL-Marine, IA, ID, IN, LA, MD, MS, MS-Marine, MT, NC, NC-Marine, NE, NJ, NY, OR, PR, RI, SD, TN, UT, VT, WA, WI, WY
Draft Audit Reports— Report to be issued 12/2000	IL, MA, NH, WV
Draft Audit Reports— Report to be issued 3/2001	MI
On-Going Fieldwork	DC, KY, ME, ME-Marine, MN, MO, NV, NM, ND, NMI, OK, PA, SC, SC-MAR, TX, VI

Trends and Weaknesses Noted in Completed and Ongoing Audits

License Issues
Eliminating duplicate licenses, problems in collecting license revenue (58%)

Accounting Systems
Reconciliations between systems, inadequate systems, poor audit trails (70%)

Expenditure Accounting
Grant versus project level accounting (13%)

Labor Systems
Weaknesses in time and activity reporting (83%)

Program Income
Tracking/accounting for program income (50%)

In-Kind Match
Inconsistencies in using in-kind match (23%)

New legislation
Placing States in diversion and does not return revenues to the program (10%)

Leases/MOU's
Allowing loss of control over assets and funding ineligible activities (17%)

Out-of-Period Costs
Overbilling for out-of-period costs (35%)

Subrecipients
Weaknesses in monitoring subrecipients compliance and cost overruns (13%)

Motor Pools
Excessive amounts for vehicle use charges (10%)

Potential Irregularities
Potential Hatch Act violations, investigations (24%)

Ineligible Costs
Law enforcement costs (37%)

Ineligible Activities
Lands purchased with FA funds used as park lands

Incompatible Land Uses
Wildlife conservation (10%)

Property and Equipment
Inadequate inventory records (27%)

FSR's
Financial reporting (61%)

Diversions
Improper use of license moneys (17%)

Federal Aid Grant Training Program

The National Federal Aid Training Program functions as part of the Washington, D.C. Office of Migratory Birds and State Programs, Federal Aid Division. The training program develops and delivers grants management training for U.S. Fish and Wildlife Service Federal Aid staff and State wildlife agency grantees.

Our training courses increase the knowledge, skills, and abilities of State and Federal personnel who administer Sport Fish and Wildlife Restoration grants. This training helps to ensure that Federal Aid grant managers consistently apply the laws, rules, and policies that govern Federal Aid grant program administration.

Approximately 250 individuals have completed the Basic Grants Management Course since it was first offered in 1996. Approximately 350 individuals have completed courses developed by or offered in cooperation with the Federal Aid Training Program.

The demand for courses continues to grow. Currently, The Service schedules Basic Grants Management courses twice each year. Since the Project Leaders Course pilot in March 2000, interest and demand for the State specific Federal Aid Project Leaders Course has grown. Current information shows that at least 24 States are interested in training for almost 700 project leaders in calendar year 2001. We customize the course to meet State's needs. We have developed a Project Leaders Course Planning Guide to help States and Federal Aid Regional Office staff in planning, developing, and delivering project leader training.

Efforts to develop additional courses for Federal Aid grant managers are in progress. Currently we are developing a course for Federal Aid fiscal managers and a compliance issues course.

Course descriptions, an on-line application, training materials, and grant manager's resources are available on Federal Aid's Training Program internet site at: http://www.nctc.fws.gov/fedaid/fatrain.htm

Federal Aid Information Management System (FAIMS)

Implemented in 1999, this computer system allows the Federal Aid Program to function uniformly throughout the nation. FAIMS facilitates the electronic transfer of grant funds to State Fish & Wildlife agencies and other grantees, through an interface with the Health and Human Service's Payment Management System (SMARTLINK). FAIMS also, since July, 2000, provides financial data to the Service's Federal Financial System to simplify tracking, accounting and reconciliation.

Beyond an accounting for the award of program funds, FAIMS is a record repository for all action taken during the review of grants. The Service records grant accomplishments in the FAIMS database, forming the source for a variety of grant program reports. All Federal Aid offices comprise the FAIMS network. Eventually, the Service will make FAIMS available for grantees and other interested parties through a web-based electronic interface. The interface will enable grantees to submit grant applications, amendments, and input financial and accomplishment reports electronically.

Thus far, the Service has established an information network permitting standardized electronic management of the grant process and financial management procedures in conformance with OMB guidance. Data flows through this FAIMS network from all regional Federal Aid offices to one of two mirrored national master sites every hour. The two national sites exchange information every 15 minutes and daily update the regional sites. Thus, data integrity is maintained through the combination of this routine data exchange and advanced backup procedures.

FAIMS Team members include:

William Conlin
Supervisor
Arlington, VA
703/358 1843

Luther Zachary
Fish & Wildlife Biologist
Lakewood, CO
303/275 2344

Dale Beaumariage
Education Specialist

C. J. Huang
Database Administrator

Pete Hitchcock
Network Engineer

Robert Vega
Computer Specialist

Randy Flower
Fiscal Specialist
Atlanta, GA
404/679 7098

Federal Aid National Outreach Team

The Federal Aid National Outreach program consists of several coordinated efforts to convey the benefits of the Sport Fish and Wildlife Restoration Programs. The National Federal Aid Outreach Team (Team) is composed of Regional representatives and Washington Office staff, carrying out cooperative outreach activities that are national in scope.

The celebration of the 50th anniversary of the Sport Fish Restoration was a focus for Team activities in 2000. By working with the American Fisheries Society, the International Association of Fish and Wildlife Agencies, and the American Sportfishing Association, the Team generated positive media coverage highlighting the history and accomplishments of the Sport Fish Restoration Program. The anniversary celebration culminated in the release of a special edition of Fisheries Magazine, published by the American Fisheries Society, devoted to the Sport Fish Restoration Program.

Financial Review
Part A

Federal Aid Gross Program Receipts: 1996–2000 *(in millions)*

Sport Fish Restoration Program

	FY96	*FY97*	*FY98*	*FY99*	*FY00*
Gas—Motorboat	127	142	114	180	175
Gas—Small Engines	53	57	48	70	60
Fishing Equipment	98	90	95	96	105
Sonar	3	3	2	2	2
Import Duties	28	33	60	26	34
Interest	41	48	53	46	42
Adjustments	0	4	0	0	0
Total Gross Receipts	350	377	372	420	418

Wildlife Restoration Program

	FY96	*FY97*	*FY98*	*FY99*	*FY00*
Pistols—Revolvers	40	35	39	40	41
Firearms	74	64	72	76	82
Ammunition	48	49	54	72	75
Bows & Arrows	18	20	15	19	17
Total Gross Receipts	180	168	180	207	215

Final Apportionment—Sport Fish Restoration, Fiscal Year 2000

Federal Aid in Sport Fish Restoration funds for Fiscal Year 2000

STATE	DOLLARS	STATE	DOLLARS
ALABAMA	3,607,904	NEVADA	3,698,911
ALASKA	12,046,916	NEW HAMPSHIRE	2,409,383
ARIZONA	5,089,496	NEW JERSEY	2,409,383
ARKANSAS	3,968,596	NEW MEXICO	4,372,502
CALIFORNIA	12,046,916	NEW YORK	6,064,107
COLORADO	6,198,128	NORTH CAROLINA	3,813,798
CONNECTICUT	2,409,383	NORTH DAKOTA	2,517,005
DELAWARE	2,409,383	OHIO	6,254,392
DISTRICT OF COLUMBIA	803,128	OKLAHOMA	4,694,058
FLORIDA	6,221,202	OREGON	5,496,382
GEORGIA	4,331,459	PENNSYLVANIA	6,046,806
HAWAII	2,409,383	RHODE ISLAND	2,409,383
IDAHO	4,114,980	SOUTH CAROLINA	3,097,296
ILLINOIS	4,963,612	SOUTH DAKOTA	3,087,681
INDIANA	3,820,091	TENNESSEE	5,408,189
IOWA	3,318,153	TEXAS	12,046,916
KANSAS	3,666,601	UTAH	4,352,260
KENTUCKY	3,486,222	VERMONT	2,409,383
LOUISIANA	4,103,273	VIRGINIA	3,928,056
MAINE	2,409,383	WASHINGTON	4,908,353
MARYLAND	2,409,383	WEST VIRGINIA	2,409,383
MASSACHUSETTS	2,409,383	WISCONSIN	8,239,191
MICHIGAN	8,544,705	WYOMING	3,870,908
MINNESOTA	8,928,236	PUERTO RICO	2,409,383
MISSISSIPPI	3,100,738	GUAM	803,128
MISSOURI	5,962,844	VIRGIN ISLANDS	803,128
MONTANA	5,579,059	AMERCAN SAMOA	803,128
NEBRASKA	3,014,134	N. MARIANA ISLANDS	803,128
		TOTAL	*240,938,312*

Final Apportionmen—Wildlife Restoration, Fiscal Year 2000

Federal Aid in Wildlife Restoration Funds for Fiscal Year 2000

State	Wildlife Restoration	Hunter Education	Total	State	Wildlife Restoration	Hunter Education	Total
ALABAMA	2,753,476	686,063	3,439,539	NEW HAMPSHIRE	819,834	292,014	1,111,848
ALASKA	8,198,344	292,014	8,490,358	NEW JERSEY	819,834	876,041	1,695,875
ARIZONA	3,965,459	622,330	4,587,789	NEW MEXICO	3,779,698	292,014	4,071,712
ARKANSAS	3,086,026	292,014	3,378,040	NEW YORK	4,848,909	876,041	5,724,950
CALIFORNIA	5,734,213	876,041	6,610,254	NORTH CAROLINA	3,277,236	876,041	4,153,277
COLORADO	4,606,451	559,365	5,165,816	NORTH DAKOTA	2,383,767	292,014	2,675,781
CONNECTICUT	819,834	558,129	1,377,963	OHIO	3,859,200	876,041	4,735,241
DELAWARE	819,834	292,014	1,111,848	OKLAHOMA	3,288,615	534,098	3,822,713
FLORIDA	2,355,999	876,041	3,232,040	OREGON	4,170,252	482,606	4,652,858
GEORGIA	3,244,337	876,041	4,120,378	PENNSYLVANIA	6,726,332	876,041	7,602,373
HAWAII	819,834	292,014	1,111,848	RHODE ISLAND	819,834	292,014	1,111,848
IDAHO	3,354,271	292,014	3,646,285	SOUTH CAROLINA	1,956,277	592,017	2,548,294
ILLINOIS	3,047,785	876,041	3,923,826	SOUTH DAKOTA	2,950,036	292,014	3,242,050
INDIANA	2,505,795	876,041	3,381,836	TENNESSEE	4,181,674	828,111	5,009,785
IOWA	2,888,304	471,473	3,359,777	TEXAS	8,198,344	876,041	9,074,385
KANSAS	3,184,828	292,014	3,476,842	UTAH	3,176,668	292,014	3,468,682
KENTUCKY	2,491,698	625,737	3,117,435	VERMONT	819,834	292,014	1,111,848
LOUISIANA	2,553,396	716,522	3,269,918	VIRGINIA	2,721,670	876,041	3,597,711
MAINE	1,855,868	292,014	2,147,882	WASHINGTON	2,886,598	826,330	3,712,928
MARYLAND	1,000,335	811,859	1,812,194	WEST VIRGINIA	2,068,602	292,014	2,360,616
MASSACHUSETTS	819,834	876,041	1,695,875	WISCONSIN	5,290,582	830,588	6,121,170
MICHIGAN	6,473,698	876,041	7,349,739	WYOMING	3,227,500	292,014	3,519,514
MINNESOTA	4,890,592	742,861	5,633,453	PUERTO RICO	819,834	0	819,834
MISSISSIPPI	2,516,454	436,914	2,953,368	GUAM	273,278	48,669	321,947
MISSOURI	4,409,095	868,843	5,277,938	VIRGIN ISLANDS	273,278	48,669	321,947
MONTANA	5,257,769	292,014	5,549,783	AMERICAN SAMOA	273,278	48,669	321,947
NEBRASKA	2,954,116	292,014	3,246,130	N. MARIANA ISLANDS	273,278	48,669	321,947
NEVADA	3,174,983	292,014	3,466,997				
				TOTAL	*163,966,870*	*29,201,362*	*193,168,232*

Number of Paid Fishing License Holders, License Sales, and Cost to Anglers, Fiscal Year 1999

State	Paid Fishing License Holders*	Resident Fishing Licenses, Tags, Permits & Stamps	Nonresident Fishing Licenses, Tags, Permits & Stamps	Total Fishing Licenses, Tags, Permits & Stamps**	Gross Cost To Anglers
ALABAMA	504,579	387,653	102,744	490,397	$6,262,990
ALASKA	410,479	253,201	381,882	635,083	12,355,338
ARIZONA	472,927	458,570	199,037	657,607	7,109,394
ARKANSAS	737,964	507,736	246,625	754,361	8,150,396
CALIFORNIA	2,109,827	2,993,482	44,509	3,037,991	46,006,433
COLORADO	760,683	501,128	436,044	937,172	11,747,590
CONNECTICUT	173,774	162,662	11,112	173,774	2,280,032
DELAWARE	24,524	25,858	4,654	30,512	246,928
FLORIDA	1,202,501	1,465,047	554,815	2,019,862	22,021,681
GEORGIA	660,425	715,394	81,648	797,042	7,024,237
HAWAII	5,937	5,900	297	6,197	20,953
IDAHO	449,535	358,118	194,750	552,868	5,989,662
ILLINOIS	763,490	795,559	38,972	834,531	9,413,745
INDIANA	617,887	576,604	89,982	666,586	5,899,635
IOWA	399,646	391,724	41,649	433,373	4,752,680
KANSAS	318,134	280,683	48,372	329,055	4,577,431
KENTUCKY	570,522	561,440	34,242	595,682	6,740,732
LOUISIANA	656,089	864,504	110,022	974,526	6,855,887
MAINE	272,528	187,647	84,881	272,528	5,798,585
MARYLAND	376,453	576,419	90,694	667,113	5,488,228
MASSACHUSETTS	173,295	334,097	17,666	351,763	4,491,569
MICHIGAN	1,322,134	1,336,938	123,994	1,460,932	22,626,857
MINNESOTA	1,548,157	1,144,388	243,045	1,387,433	23,948,702
MISSISSIPPI	419,802	399,643	86,385	486,028	4,634,870
MISSOURI	909,026	1,209,066	285,858	1,494,924	12,518,919
MONTANA	377,668	240,301	342,172	582,473	8,185,537
NEBRASKA	213,332	376,378	56,317	432,695	4,034,691
NEVADA	174,700	229,133	48,028	277,161	3,233,951
NEW HAMPSHIRE	162,702	116,705	52,436	169,141	3,624,390
NEW JERSEY	175,536	274,464	12,686	287,150	4,011,875
NEW MEXICO	228,063	171,510	103,972	275,482	4,110,000
NEW YORK	1,052,421	880,083	173,358	1,053,441	13,835,411
NORTH CAROLINA	649,430	641,914	59,496	701,410	12,122,255
NORTH DAKOTA	155,145	134,532	26,915	161,447	1,420,152
OHIO	1,168,134	1,028,863	139,271	1,168,134	15,960,621
OKLAHOMA	641,313	438,706	92,315	531,021	7,884,528
OREGON	653,351	817,772	175,471	993,243	13,717,129
PENNSYLVANIA	1,093,598	1,659,447	143,698	1,803,145	20,030,587
RHODE ISLAND	33,587	52,399	3,647	56,046	441,353
SOUTH CAROLINA	507,252	514,512	90,017	604,529	5,620,223
SOUTH DAKOTA	244,768	276,630	85,138	361,768	3,941,513
TENNESSEE	1,011,017	1,015,727	209,029	1,224,756	12,961,457
TEXAS	1,469,815	1,993,805	107,379	2,101,184	32,206,411
UTAH	457,086	550,546	287,806	838,352	8,659,450
VERMONT	101,762	84,468	49,270	133,738	2,356,510
VIRGINIA	630,374	728,133	84,179	812,312	9,158,993
WASHINGTON	692,755	1,033,298	42,330	1,075,628	14,272,969
WEST VIRGINIA	283,606	274,267	9,339	283,606	4,822,896
WISCONSIN	1,374,185	1,144,534	377,013	1,521,547	23,303,474
WYOMING	301,205	125,566	212,854	338,420	4,338,233
Totals	*29,713,123*	*31,297,154*	*6,538,015*	*37,835,169*	*$481,218,083*

* A paid license holder is one individual regardless of the number of licenses purchased.
 (Data certified by State Fish and Game Departments.)
** Persons who fished in more than one State are counted in each State where they fished.

Number of Paid Hunting License Holders, License Sales, and Cost to Hunters—FiscalYear 1999

State	Paid Hunting License Holders*	Resident Hunting Licenses, Tags, Permits & Stamps	Nonresident Hunting Licenses, Tags, Permits & Stamps	Total Hunting Licenses, Tags, Permits & Stamps**	Gross Cost To Hunters
ALABAMA	272,525	255,342	41,396	296,738	$7,217,391
ALASKA	95,745	180,825	37,550	218,375	9,281,172
ARIZONA	198,025	330,635	31,612	362,247	8,170,517
ARKANSAS	412,114	442,172	99,915	542,087	11,565,396
CALIFORNIA	309,236	827,700	11,192	838,892	14,001,052
COLORADO	328,879	342,622	216,961	559,583	41,763,556
CONNECTICUT	61,608	137,145	7,490	144,635	1,720,666
DELAWARE	21,357	31,552	3,559	35,111	515,779
FLORIDA	178,101	320,742	5,931	326,673	4,785,618
GEORGIA	332,635	824,249	62,164	886,413	11,851,483
HAWAII	9,346	9,611	199	9,810	158,179
IDAHO	250,243	790,403	90,890	881,293	17,545,606
ILLINOIS	308,662	1,107,208	36,597	1,143,805	12,759,852
INDIANA	300,732	631,832	19,238	651,070	8,269,440
IOWA	275,780	749,807	112,597	862,404	13,279,223
KANSAS	209,734	384,144	63,859	448,003	10,411,806
KENTUCKY	280,991	697,260	42,948	740,208	10,053,707
LOUISIANA	271,541	588,158	27,394	615,552	7,254,129
MAINE	207,004	166,147	40,857	207,004	6,060,250
MARYLAND	135,436	185,956	35,184	221,140	4,421,913
MASSACHUSETTS	74,241	237,013	4,759	241,772	2,432,062
MICHIGAN	920,473	2,387,595	42,772	2,430,367	25,041,257
MINNESOTA	555,926	1,153,208	18,676	1,171,884	20,658,676
MISSISSIPPI	250,035	244,778	43,848	288,626	8,073,645
MISSOURI	505,662	1,073,156	47,717	1,120,873	16,939,290
MONTANA	280,382	603,845	119,833	723,678	20,454,823
NEBRASKA	186,452	353,847	67,147	420,994	7,681,904
NEVADA	59,501	89,515	11,568	101,083	2,946,538
NEW HAMPSHIRE	78,328	232,467	30,053	262,520	3,247,139
NEW JERSEY	89,460	273,377	8,027	281,404	6,443,337
NEW MEXICO	103,990	204,735	36,509	241,244	10,770,000
NEW YORK	698,844	1,605,422	63,852	1,669,274	18,561,868
NORTH CAROLINA	399,043	479,350	24,727	504,077	8,922,305
NORTH DAKOTA	116,664	353,657	96,452	450,109	5,199,602
OHIO	519,996	1,191,414	14,232	1,205,646	15,870,784
OKLAHOMA	296,548	312,796	10,729	323,525	7,139,770
OREGON	318,133	1,399,516	56,495	1,456,011	16,993,574
PENNSYLVANIA	1,071,955	2,391,452	129,104	2,520,556	25,769,926
RHODE ISLAND	11,704	32,005	2,895	34,900	280,526
SOUTH CAROLINA	263,045	208,937	57,560	266,497	6,702,225
SOUTH DAKOTA	204,599	327,535	81,522	409,057	10,308,607
TENNESSEE	613,654	805,872	37,598	843,470	13,695,430
TEXAS	978,837	1,183,461	55,072	1,238,533	24,234,375
UTAH	190,092	375,328	19,090	394,418	10,709,788
VERMONT	103,629	178,104	29,723	207,827	3,600,912
VIRGINIA	317,939	786,044	45,481	831,525	11,129,908
WASHINGTON	286,188	737,516	6,865	744,381	11,535,863
WEST VIRGINIA	282,195	238,434	43,761	282,195	10,533,628
WISCONSIN	769,430	2,507,324	121,583	2,628,907	35,535,724
WYOMING	136,736	174,422	66,821	241,243	17,755,790
Totals	*15,143,375*	*31,145,635*	*2,382,004*	*33,527,639*	*$580,256,011*

* A paid license holder is one individual regardless of the number of licenses purchased.
 (Data certified by State Fish and Game Departments.)
** Persons who hunted in more than one State are counted in each State where they hunted.

Deductions for Administration (*Including GAS*)

Fiscal Years	Wildlife Restoration Program			Sport Fish Restoration Program	
	Amount	*Percent* [1]		*Amount* [2]	*Percent* [1]
1939-76	$35,184,124			$12,776,627	
1977 [3]	5,287,154	5.9		1,784,610	6.7
1978	4,889,316	7.2		2,031,887	7.7
1979	3,818,633	4.1		1,369,505	4.8
1980	4,974,102	5.3		2,417,772	7.9
1981	7,250,651	7.9		2,690,051	8.0
1982	4,927,999	4.0		1,973,626	6.2
1983	4,394,029	3.9		2,201,798	6.3
1984	5,256,702	5.6		2,325,466	5.9
1985	6,772,254	7.9		3,025,995	7.9
1986	8,528,516	7.1		7,267,378	5.9
1987	6,487,540	5.9		5,855,884	4.2
1988	5,189,251	5.9		5,373,398	4.2
1989	7,534,070	6.0		7,162,802	3.8
1990	9,994,000	7.9		10,391,000	5.4
1991	13,683,734	8.0		12,541,280	5.9
1992	9,958,217	6.2		12,514,431	5.8
1993	11,888,000	7.5		11,714,000	5.2
1994	11,297,000	6.2		10,573,000	5.7
1995	14,012,598	6.3		12,750,084	6.0
1996	14,326,972	6.6		12,583,206	6.0
1997	14,357,737	8.0		15,473,218	5.4
1998	13,461,598	8.0		17,363,518	6.0
1999	14,378,562	8.0		13,559,307	6.0
2000	13,536,368	6.5		15,379,041	6.0
Totals	$251,389,127			$203,098,884	

[1] *Maximum deduction: 8% for Wildlife; 6% for Sport Fish. The Wallop-Breaux Amendment of 1984, which took effect in 1986, limited Sport Fish deductions to 6%. Prior to the Amendment, the maximum was 8%.*

[2] *Deductions for Sport Fish Restoration began in 1952.*

[3] *FY 1977 includes funding for the Transition Quarter.*

Financial Review
Part B

Fiscal Year 2000 Actual Gross Receipts

Wildlife Restoration
(in millions)

Category	FY 96	FY 97	FY 98	FY 99	FY 00
Pistols	$40	$35	$39	$40	$41
Firearms	74	64	72	75	82
Amo	48	49	54	73	75
Bows/A	18	20	15	19	17
Total	$180	$168	$180	$207	$215

Comments:
- *All figures are actuals.*
- *Apportionments are calculated on the above gross receipts.*

Fiscal Year 2000 Actual Gross Receipts

Sport Fish Restoration
(in millions)

Category	FY 96	FY 97	FY 98	FY 99	FY 00
Gas MB	$127	$142	$114	$180	$175
Gas S.Eng	53	57	48	70	60
Fish Equip	98	90	95	96	105
Sonar	3	3	2	2	2
Imports	28	33	60	26	34
Interest	41	48	53	46	42
Total	$350	$373	$372	$420	$418

Comments:
- *All figures are actuals.*
- *Apportionments are calculated on the above gross receipts.*

Federal Aid Cash Management

Status of Investments and Interest Earned, Fiscal Year 2000

Wildlife Restoration Program

Balance	Investments	Interest Earned
Sept 30, 1999	$ 840,000,000	$ 19,142,459
Sept 30, 2000	860,833,000	19,165,391

Sport Fish Restoration

Balance	Investments	Interest Earned
Sept 30, 1999	$ 1,065,434,641	$ 45,961,362
Sept 30, 2000	1,150,551,771	41,884,186

Summary—Total Balances as Sept 30, 2000

Balance	Investments	Interest Earned
Wildlife Restoration	$ 860,833,000	$19,165,391
Sport Fish Restoration	1,150,551,771	41,884,186
Total	$ 2,011,384,771	$61,049,577

Federal Aid Cash Management Analysis of FY 2000 Transactions
(in millions)

Transaction	Wildlife Restoration	Sport Fish Restoration
Balance: Sept 30, 1999	$ 840	$ 1,065
Receipts	215	418
Total	$ 1055	$ 1,483
Disbursements: Oct 99–Sept 00		
Federal Aid/States	$ (195)	$ (259)
Corps of Engineers	0	(23)
Coast Guard	0	(51)
North American	0	(4)
Total	$ (195)	$ (337)
Balance: Sept 30, 2000	*$ 860*	*$ 1,146*

Federal Aid Cash Management

Investments, Interest Earned and Cash Transfers to States 1996–2000
(Dollar amounts in millions)

Fiscal Year	Investments			Interest Earned			Cash Transfers to States		
Wildlife	*Sport Fish*		*Total*	*Wildlife*	*Sport Fish*	*Total*	*Via Banks*	*No. of Transfers*	*Amount Amount*
1996	$456	$745	$1,201	$24	$41	$65	98	2411	$410
1997	397	865	1,262	24	47	71	99	2484	417
1998	417	945	1,362	25	53	78	99	2498	441
1999	840	1,065	1,905	19	46	65	99	2479	559
2000	860	1,151	2,011	19	42	61	99	2495	546

U.S. Department of the Interior
U.S. Fish & Wildlife Service
Division of Federal Aid

http://www.fws.gov